WOMAN
Is Not a Dirty Word

by
Amy Olson-Treptow

PublishAmerica
Baltimore

© 2006 by Amy Olson-Treptow.
All rights reserved. No part of this book may be reproduced, stored in a retrieval system or transmitted in any form or by any means without the prior written permission of the publishers, except by a reviewer who may quote brief passages in a review to be printed in a newspaper, magazine or journal.

First printing

At the specific preference of the author, PublishAmerica allowed this work to remain exactly as the author intended, verbatim, without editorial input.

ISBN: 1-4241-2896-X
PUBLISHED BY PUBLISHAMERICA, LLLP
www.publishamerica.com
Baltimore

Printed in the United States of America

Contents

Foreword 5
Preface 9
Dedications 11
Acknowledgments 13
Introduction 15
Opening… 17
Woman Is Not a Dirty Word 20
Characteristics Unbecoming a Lady 23
Friends from a Distance 26
Unpredictable, Yet, So Predictable 29
Temper, Temper 33
More Than One Treatment 36
Why Do You Need It? 41
Really, Woman Isn't a Dirty Word? 45
Lie to Me 47
Finally, Diagnosis 51
It's All-Good 57
What Have I Done? 60
Life After Treatment 62
Thankful 67
Post Script 71
References 73
Notes 75

Foreword

Bipolar Disorder impacts approximately one percent of the population at any given time. It typically presents during adolescence or early adulthood – although diagnosis may be delayed for years due to the challenges in diagnosis.

Bipolar Disorder or *Manic Depression* includes symptoms of recurrent episodes of moderate to severe depression with episodic episodes of grossly elevated and expansive mood. In addition to mood instability, symptoms may include sleep difficulties, elevated or low energy, decreased concentration and motivation, agitation, lack of enjoyment of activities, engaging in activities that may have a negative consequence, hopelessness, and suicidal ideation. These changes in mood typically cause marked impairment and dysfunction in relationships with others, occupational disabilities, and financial stress.

Family studies have demonstrated a genetic factor in the development of Bipolar Disorder. First-degree relatives of those diagnosed with Bipolar Disorder have a much greater probability of developing Bipolar Disorder or a mood disorder themselves. The prevalence of mood disorders is not impacted by race or socioeconomic status.

Patients with Bipolar Disorder often have other psychiatric disorders such as anxiety and chemical dependency or complicating medical disorders. In addition to the struggle of living with significant mood altering symptoms it may prevent people from engaging in daily activities that most people take for granted such as relationships with family and friends, occupational endeavors, and social activities. The obvious morbidity of Bipolar Disorder is high – but mortality issues are concerning with reported suicide rates as high as twenty percent.

Treatment modalities include pharmacotherapy and individual and group psychotherapy. Hospitalization is not uncommon and is warranted to assure patient safety in specific situations. Family members receive support through family support groups and educational programs.

Ms. Olson-Treptow's book, *Woman is Not a Dirty Word*, describes her own passage through depression and eventual diagnosis of Bipolar Disorder. These chapters describe her chronic and long-standing experiences with mood instability and the recent understanding of the origin of them and hopeful stabilization of her symptoms.

Kathryn D. Lombardo, MD
Chair of the Department of Psychiatry and Psychology
Olmsted Medical Center
Rochester, Minnesota

Hope is powerful if you have it and essential if you don't...

Preface

I speak openly about several people from both my present and past in this book. Much has changed since the time I've encountered many of them. Please take into consideration that both they and I have since moved on and (with hope) learned greatly from past experiences. Also, parts of this book relate to instances prior to treatment as an adult or any therapy. Interspersed there are current journal entries to note that my journey with Bipolar Disorder (BD) continues. Please know that there are other issues besides BD that contribute to some of the experiences written about here as well.

I had reservations about sharing some aspects of my life through this book. I feel strongly though, that this information is too powerful to be swept under the rug. If, after reading the book, people have a certain perception of someone with Bipolar Disorder, I hope that it is a positive one. I also hope that it brings an understanding of what is yet to come from me.

I begin the book by discussing different symptoms of being bipolar: manic episodes, depressive symptoms, suicidal thoughts, erratic behavior, and the eventual complete loss of interest in daily activities. I can honestly say that I hope my most recent suicide attempt was my last. Therapy and medications do work if given the chance.

Finally, because of when I was raised (throughout the late 1970's, 1980's, and early 1990's) and the locations where I grew up, the options for treatment of Bipolar Disorder, which exist today, didn't back then. Resources and research for Bipolar Disorder have come a long way, yet, there is much left to discover.

Dedications

To my parents, Loren and Jacky, who've suffered with me,
to my brothers, JoWayne and Loren Jr., who've thankfully been my friends,
to my husband, Chad, who continues to be my constant supporter,
and to my children, Carter and Spencer, whom I adore.

Acknowledgments

I've never been so happy to feel "crazy" in my life! After a too long and hard struggle, I can honestly thank the teachers, counselors, therapists and doctors who've come into my life for the past 20 years. I owe them my gratitude for showing me that Bipolar Disorder is more than the extremes of being stoic, then overly emotional, and then stoic again. It brings new meaning to the phrase, "things happen for a reason." I'm able to share my experiences with others who feel like their mind is not their own.

I'm grateful for the opportunity to express myself through this book as well as being able to speak with others personally about manic depression. I encourage people to talk about how they feel. If not with a professional, with a trusted loved one (I hope they're out there for you!). I also hope to inspire people to listen when being spoken to. The experiences, which are shared in this book, are meant to be learned from. For that, I thank my parents. I no longer have to question my existence.

I also want to thank my immediate family for bringing out the best and worst in me. Without them, I would not know my limitations, or my potential.

Introduction

From its title, it sounds like this is a book regarding feminist ideology or women's rights. Being female, it's inevitable that there wouldn't be some aspect of these experienced. However, this isn't a book about feminism or the like. It's a book about my experiences with manic depression (later termed Bipolar Disorder by psychiatrists and occasionally referred to as BD in this book).

Bipolar Disorder is more than just having a flat affect in the morning, wearing frumpy and uncoordinated, then greatly inappropriate, clothing in the afternoon, or speaking out of turn when manic, only to become suicidal later in the day. It's like having been molested as a child. You become robbed of your spirit. You want people to say, "You're not alone," "It's not your fault," "I believe you," "I'm sorry you're going through this." Instead, what you may receive is "What excuse is that for your behavior" or an emphatic "Yeah, right." And that's if you have the courage to tell people about your too often suicidal or homicidal thoughts/feelings at all.

My life was changed the day I was diagnosed with BD and began taking the correct medications. Finally I knew why I had sudden mood changes so frequently; why I overreacted to minor situations and made incidences out of nothing; and why I was so jittery, agitated, and overwhelmed when there was no reason to be. Everything and nothing was the matter. I was constantly looking at the big, broad picture (using words like always and never) instead of taking things one-step at a time. I needed a defined identity and control (a specific job title, keeping my maiden name after marriage, and not only being on volunteer committees but chairing them/being a member of the executive board for example). Perfectionism, not finding the good in anything, being overly cynical or critical, and not being grateful for what I had were common. I might have an impressive resume', but the price my psyche' has paid is irrevocable.

I'm not writing this information to hurt anyone. I can only tell people what I've experienced. I think you'll see within this book a common thread that ties together what someone with Bipolar Disorder, Type II, experiences with the existing material written by those who diagnose it. It's more than going into an emotional tailspin after a bad haircut (one that you described to the stylist because you thought it would look great on you) then feeling overwhelmed because you've again gone from one extreme to another (from foot-long hair to practically shaven for example.) It's like having overly simplistic thoughts and not knowing how to describe them (as if self-doubt wasn't enough).

My hope is that someone who suspects they have manic depression reads these words and finds solace in knowing that it's not the end of their world. There is life with BD. It takes a great understanding of yourself as well as the disorder to live "happily ever after" though…

Opening...

Everybody's got issues. It's unfortunate how long it takes some folks to realize that they're not special. Ever since I can remember, though, I was special. Not because anyone told me so. I just knew. As a child I would consider myself special simply because I had a new pair of shoes that nobody else had or because my mother made my clothes (no one else's mom did that for them!) When asked what my plans were upon graduation from high school I responded by saying, "to rule the world." *How inflated was my ego?* For some reason, I had an "us versus them" mentality. I had no qualms with anyone in particular but surely I was better than so many other people! Being judgmental was my specialty. Now, but for the grace of God go I.

It didn't occur to me until college that some people might not want to hear my opinion. Like a foreigner unused to a new language, I kept on speaking obliviously. Ideas of grandeur are common. Smooth transition is difficult. I jump from one subject to another rapidly. People have told me to slow down, "You're talking too fast" or have asked, "What are you talking about?" when my conversation isn't following with theirs. It's as if I'm not making any sense, yet, in my own mind I'm brilliant. Lord knows that simply because you're high functioning, that doesn't make you sane. *Surly I can't be the only one who thinks this way?*

It's interesting to feel unique or weird; to stand out from the crowd, even if it's for the wrong reasons. Having Bipolar Disorder makes you feel unique and weird. It's hard to describe. You place expectations upon yourself that other people wouldn't (anything less than an "A" means failure). You feel you should be able to accomplish impossible tasks. You don't ask for help because you feel like you're able to do everything yourself although nothing is ever good enough. And you think that other people are constantly judging you. *Maybe they are? — Is paranoia a symptom of being bipolar?* — When you have a mood disorder, fluctuation isn't good.

Going from one end of a spectrum to another, you don't see gray, only black or white. There is no middle ground; yet, you can't make a decision because you're sitting on the fence with each extreme. Even if you know something is wrong, you don't feel morally corrupt for having had meaningless sex with multiple partners, an abortion or two, an affair with a married man; or other like sins for that matter. You only hope that if you do have children some day, that they don't inherit Bipolar Disorder. I wouldn't wish it upon my worst enemy. It's like going from the great heights of heaven to the abyss of a black hole within a matter of seconds.

There are good things about being bipolar, however. You get what you see. You tend not to tease because it seems too intimate. Whether it's not being able to smile for a friend's wedding pictures (even though I was in the wedding) or making a complete fool of myself by being the life of the party during a manic phase—no alcohol required; the emotion is always real. It's like the constant struggle of having to stroke your own ego (not caring how anyone else feels) and walking on eggshells, hoping that no one else will notice how rude you're being.

There are times, though, that I become physically exhausted after a manic phase and emotionally drained after a severe depression. I worry about things that need not be worried over. I don't want to have anything to do with a beloved pet or even my own children. It becomes too difficult to pay attention. Impatience is obvious. I jump in to finish other people's sentences because they can't keep up with my racing mind. Yet, in jumping in, I'm completely off regarding what they were about to say and I have to repeatedly ask the same question because the answer has escaped me within two seconds of hearing it. I feel the need to speak even if no one wants to hear what I have to say. Selfish thoughts take over. My sarcasm is as inviting as a warm, dirty diaper. Songs on the radio play like a broken tape recorder, first fast forward, then too slowly to keep up with my mind. I'm more easily annoyed than usual. Now I'm just being mean. I look at a clock for the time and wonder why I needed to know it in the first place and then forget (again) what time it was. There is a constant feeling that I'm forgetting something. *Maybe there is a need to re-live moments? Is ADHD another symptom? Why does shit need to be so difficult?* Even though my head hurts I don't reach for the pain reliever because it's too tempting to overdose. I let people use me and don't feel taken advantage of. I'm also known for doing something I have no recollection of doing. Then the cycle begins again.

Woman Is Not a Dirty Word

Up until the age of 25 (when I married), I believed that in order to discuss anything regarding the words woman, girl, or female was forbidden unless you were a self-proclaimed feminist. There are so many negative connotations associated with being female: "You throw like a girl" or "you cry/gossip/whine like a schoolgirl." The words bitch, witch, cunt, hooker, slut, whore, and hussy assumes solely a blasphemous female (or a dog in heat – really flattering). The only time the word woman is actually used is when people are describing something very serious [statistics of women who are being studied or a disease incidence rate for example]. Otherwise we typically see women in the public eye who've been successful merely by their looks or by using their sexuality (unless they're politicians, and that usually isn't an issue.) I mean, it's great that we applaud women who've made it big by flaunting what they've got. All females pay the price of objectivity, however (pornography, prostitution, sexual assault, not being treated as equals, etc.)

As a child, I recall feeling powerless against almost everything. My older brother used to hit me or holler at me out of the blue whenever he became frustrated. One day Mom stood us beside one another and said to me, "Hit him back." I couldn't do it. She grabbed my hand and repeated; "Hit him back," motioning towards him. Again I just stood there and cowered. I didn't have the momentum or the urge to seek revenge. Like a stray dog that'd been kicked too many times I just gave up on myself. Mom shook her head in disbelief and said, "You're going to have to learn to stick up for yourself. You can't rely on your looks to get you through life you know." I know Mom meant well and can be a great advocate when she believes in something strongly enough, but this didn't improve my confidence.

My parents are complete opposites. Dad is as passive and contained as Mom is flamboyant and outspoken. When Dad does speak, he calls women Herefords or heifers. He also prides himself on being called a dirty old man. Dad isn't much on flattery for women since Mom filed for divorce. Even before then, though, he wasn't exactly chivalrous (of course neither was his father before him). I think it took the divorce of Dad's brother to make him realize that women truly didn't appreciate such nicknames. This isn't news to most people, but I'm not related to most people.

Growing up, there were also several instances where people around me were putting down women. The fact that Dad didn't stick up for me (as a female) greatly affected how I saw men and how I was supposed to be treated by them. If you already have an emotional disturbance, this seems subtle, but it's huge. I was already feeling inadequate as a girl; did I also have to feel so worthless as person?

My maternal grandfather was also less than chivalrous. He had a crude sense of humor. When my step dad (Mom's fourth husband) asked Grandpa for her hand in marriage his response was, "Are you sure you don't want a clean girl?"

That's not to say that my dad or grandfathers were always bad influences or that I didn't have any positive male role models in my life. They've had to learn how to treat women with respect (as do many others). But if you've never been taught, then you can't be expected to learn. On the other hand, there are some things women do that make men question their need for chivalry...

Characteristics Unbecoming a Lady

So many flaws can be blamed on Bipolar Disorder. Character flaws like lying, bragging, flaunting, divisiveness, and cheating cannot always be included, however. Being tacky, lazy, stubborn, unforgiving, insensitive, taking advantage of situations, having a supiority complex, being obnoxious, and making everything about you are close seconds. Every symptom associated with being bipolar is a normal emotion with the exception of feeling suicidal or homicidal. It's the extremes that are difficult.

Not everyone becomes so giddy that they laugh hysterically at trivial occurrences or so sad that they can't bear to get out of bed. Quirks are having a sweet tooth or watching repeat episodes of your favorite TV show because you know what's going to happen, not having suicidal ideology. What are hard to differentiate are instances like driving. My motto used to be (and occasionally still is), "It's get the hell out of my way day, didn't you get the memo?" I know road rage is all too frequent, but people just piss me off! I'm now the idiot behind you doing exactly what I've just cussed you out for doing.—Trying to give someone the finger with your mitten on when it's cold out is not only frustrating, but also, moot. My point is that we can blame so many things on a disorder, but they're not all tied in. It can't be: I'm bipolar, she's bipolar, wouldn't you like to be bipolar too? Simply because you fluctuate in moods from one day to another doesn't mean you're bipolar. Trust me, you'll have no doubt when/if you're ever diagnosed.

It bites to have a victim's mentality and a defeatist attitude (I'm not good enough, smart enough, pretty enough, nobody likes me anyways, etc.) I end up having to pick myself up emotionally and dust my soul off for a conscience. Manic depression also makes me question my true personality. For example, when I was out of work I'd ask myself, am I a perfectionist in search of the ideal job that doesn't exist or am I just being lazy today?

I used to lack the confidence to do anything productive and would question my ability and the results if I did. There came a point in time, though, that I no longer cared if I was doing well or not. And when I'd say, "I don't care," it literally meant, "I don't care!" When you get there, that can be a tenuous place. Even though I'd thrive on attention, I didn't believe I was worthy of it. Being self-centered is inevitable, however, when you unconsciously want it:

- I once very publicly ostracized a woman for declining a bachelorette party the evening before her wedding.
- I hollered at a store clerk simply for asking me for identification.
- I bawled out a friend in front of others in our neighborhood for giving my telephone number to a photographer as a referral.
- I used to make certain absolutely nothing on my plate would touch (to the amazement of others).
- I humiliated a co-worker for talking to a friend while on the job.
- I drove a woman to quit and have made certain that others have lost their jobs because of minor mistakes.

I could go on but I believe you get the just of it. Most people would become slightly annoyed and let such instances go. The fact that I have to be right is burdensome. It also isn't good for relationships…

Friends from a Distance

"Friends" are only good if you trust them whether you're related to them or not:

November 27, 2005

Sure, everybody's been screwed over at some point in time, but why can't I trust anyone? I know why. It'll backfire. It's been proven time and again. As soon as I confide in someone, they're ready to gossip. Maybe it's a natural impulse? I know I love to hear about somebody else's pitfalls, as long as they're not my own...

I feel this need to keep friends at a distance, several notable people who I can drop a line to in a Christmas card every year until they die. There aren't any I truly trust though. There might be one or two whom I possibly can? But I'm not willing to take that chance. Even if someone extends an olive branch, forgiveness seems moot. The trust just isn't there.

Mom wonders why I treat her family members like they're pariah? I haven't spoken to Aunt Cathie since 1996. I confided in her and she betrayed me big-time. After she told everyone about Roger [older cousin] inappropriately touching me when I was pre-pubescent, I can't look any of them in the face. I'm ashamed that they now know and question whether they believe me. Besides, I hate to see how they treat Mom. Despite everything she has done to them and continues to do to me (intentionally or unintentionally), I can't stand to see her hurt.

I can still be cordial to people who I believe have screwed me over. It's good manners. Not only have I been kind to those who've been less than kind to me, I've been affable to people who didn't deserve the time of day. It sickens me to remember when one of the people who'd molested me as a child came and sat with my father and me at a drive-in restaurant. We were outside sitting on a picnic table when he approached us. He sat down and began talking with Dad. I felt hot in the face and wanted to hurl. Instead I just stared at him and agreed to whatever he was talking with Dad about. He was only there for a few seconds, but I didn't say a word to Dad about the incident that was upsetting me. Maybe that's why it's easier to just avoid people in the first place? Like seeing an old classmate on the street or at the county fair, I tended to avoid them too. Not only was it easier, I didn't have to feel pressured into lying about any success I had or didn't have. Then again, what did I have to prove? *There's such a need to impress others for some reason.*

As a teenager you feel invincible and therefore can easily impress others (or so I thought). Between the ages of thirteen and sixteen I put my parents through hell. I brought home men twice my age who were jobless, used drugs, had a criminal record, or just plain would have made ugly grandchildren. I wrecked more than one vehicle. I stayed out all night without word as to my whereabouts, took many a pregnancy test, bleached my hair with peroxide and cut it very short myself, and was stopped more than once by the police for moving violations (always fun when you live in a small town).

My cousin, who is nine months my senior, and I would consistently get into trouble together. We'd carouse the streets looking for excitement. Unfortunately we found it. I remember how we'd buy cigarettes (before you had to be eighteen), call some guy for a ride, and cruise around town to kill boredom. We'd sneak out, be picked up by someone, holler out the window at passers-by, and maybe stop to knock on someone's house door and run before they caught us. We'd make prank phone calls to people we randomly selected through the phone book and would charge long distance calls to the neighbor through three-way calling. We'd stay up until all hours of the night, climb out onto the roof of the house, or just walk around town and swear at people to see what kind of reaction we'd get. We once bummed a ride to a neighboring community to go to a county fair, and then ditched the guys who brought us. We had to call our parents for a ride home when the fair shut down for the evening. Needless to say, she ended up pregnant at thirteen and I lost my virginity shortly thereafter. My point is, we used to do everything together. It's like the relationship you have with your siblings before they have a significant other to take your place. No matter how close you are to someone, things change. I love my cousin and always will. But no matter how close we used to be as kids, I just don't have the ability to fully trust her (or anyone else) as an adult.

Unpredictable, Yet, So Predictable

Good, bad, or indifferent, people judge you by your relatives. I see similarities between me and mine and it scares the hell out of me! For example, the uncouth act of talking on the phone while sitting on the toilet or pointing out other people's eccentricities. I finally concluded that you don't have to have a great relationship with everyone you're related to. I'm easily annoyed anyhow. Why push it? I remember recording a journal entry regarding my mother:

September 6, 2005

I'm disappointed, disgusted, angry, embarrassed, feel taken for granted, ashamed, inadequate, and am sick of being treated like I'm an idiot who'll believe anything. If I had only one wish it wouldn't be for fame or fortune, it would be that my mother stops lying. She's a compulsive liar. This greatly contributes to my depression. These feelings have almost driven me again to suicide. Every significant relationship Mom has had (her parents, 4 siblings, 4 husbands, 2 fiancées between the husbands, and 3 children) has either been destroyed or greatly compromised by her lies or inability to cope with the truth. This compromises my relationships with those same individuals. I've spent years defending her "exaggerations." The final straw came when she claimed to be a Hurricane Katrina survivor at our garage sale last weekend. There is no honor left to defend. I believe she can be truly shameless.

About 35 years ago she could blame her parents for her life choices; but there is no excuse for her behavior now. My grandparents may be blamed for not instilling character, respect, dignity, trust, or integrity; but as a grown woman, you'd think Mom would've picked up on some of these traits.

Mom saw a psych doctor for a brief period of time and was making progress. She said he was helpful but was just "too busy" for her and stopped going. I believe it just got too real. I suggested she find another therapist. That was about a year ago. Mom doesn't have health insurance so this contributes to the problem. I sincerely want my mother to be happy...genuinely happy (versus playing dumb).

Mom doesn't seem to realize the fact that many of her bad experiences in life stem from her poor decisions and lies. She continues to make questionable decisions on a daily basis. Yet, when she asks for your opinion or suggestions, they're usually met with an excuse as to why it won't work. It's difficult to take anything Mom says seriously.

I try very hard not to be like my mother (not to be mean, but out of fear of making some of the same mistakes – especially with my own children). She'll tell anecdotes about when I was a child and it's very upsetting to me. First, because I don't know if I can believe what she's saying and second because I had frequent miserable moments in childhood that I remember vividly (her hitting me over the head with a saucepan, throwing a glass vase at me, hollering at me for "ruining" her chili by draining canned vegetable water into it, amongst other things). Although she has good traits, I don't feel I should have to look so hard to find them. She's correct when she says, "I may not have done everything right, but I didn't do everything wrong either." Then again, she often quotes other people and tries to take credit for it.

I use sarcasm and silence as defenses. My brothers use avoidance. Both moved out of state as soon as possible. I used to dread getting phone calls from Mom because I knew I'd be lied to. There was a brief amount of time where we had great conversations. But somehow things have gotten back to where I dread the phone calls again. Maybe my expectations are too high? I don't expect the perfect mother. However, one of these years it would be nice to be as proud of Mom as she is of me. I'm tired of "walking on eggshells" so she won't be upset. Yet, I don't want to pick a fight (fight vs. flight) in order to resolve hurt feelings. She tends to turn conversations into something different and altogether unintended.

There are so many contributing factors to Mom's behavior. Her physical, emotional, and sexual abuse as a child, her life decisions, and her finances are just a few. Compulsive overeating and overspending are also key. She recently declared bankruptcy despite her husband's wishes. As owner-operators (truck drivers) she and her husband were making great money as team drivers. Two years ago she talked about finding a different line of work, yet she kept spending as if money were no object. Now that their house is being sold, she wants sympathy and, I believe, undue attention. She's an adult. She "signed on the dotted line" to buy the house, a camper, a trailer, and 2 new trucks (one a semi). I don't want her to blow it with her husband. He's the only one I've considered a Step-Dad (vs. just another husband). I get mad when I think about all the items purchased over the years (magazines, knick-knacks, "collectibles", exorbitant amounts of decorations, clothing, jewelry, multiple unneeded/repeat items, bulk food, etc.) that could've gone towards my college education (instead of me having to take out huge student loans).

My intension is not to "beat up" on Mom by pointing out flaws. I would like for her to be able to rise above certain situations and be proud of herself (in a non-egotistical way.)—Instead of complaining, belittling, or being constantly negative, it would be nice to have her experience true joy instead of playing the game of one-up-man ship. If my mother knew how to be completely honest with herself, I think the other aspects of her life would fall into place.

Mom can be the most fun, vibrant, jubilant, spontaneous, and generous person. However, the consequences of her actions aren't thought out in advance and are hurting the people she says she loves the *most. I'm not sure where to even begin a conversation about her story telling, no, blatant lies? I just know that it is very difficult to respect her when you know she is making a fool of herself. I'm afraid to talk to my mother because of her denial of reality and her temper. Sometimes I feel like I need to be a licensed therapist to have a conversation with her. I'm 32. Mom is 53. I've heard that all of a woman's relationships are based upon the mother-daughter relationship. I have no sisters so it would be nice to have a decent relationship with her. However, lately I'm wondering why I bother letting her into my life at all. I'll share this journal entry with Mom some day. I think she will be surprised, yet, I'll wonder why it hasn't been more obvious to her. Just when you think she's getting her life in order, she somehow jeopardizes it, and it is always someone else's fault (accountability is nonexistent). I also realize that I can't use her as a scapegoat for my own feelings.*

I hear, "You teach people how to treat you." You also get what you give. We're both long overdue for resolution. It bothers me when she talks about imaginary conversations she's had with relatives (her aunts/siblings/sisters-in-law usually) or famous people. Even partial-truths are hard to take.

I wish that all of this information would've come out when I was 12. I didn't know how to express myself then but it has gotten easier over the years. I can't blame Mom & Dad for every wrong decision I've made in life. I sure wish I'd have had proper guidance, however. Regret is a powerful emotion.

Now if that's not bipolar behavior (both hers and mine), then I'm not sure how else to describe it? There is no question in my mind that I've inherited BD.

Temper, Temper

December 12, 2005

Something inside me snaps if I'm rubbed the wrong way. I tend to get ticked off more than others. I'm not dangerous, although, I could be. That's what's frightening. I don't think I'm a classic textbook case of someone with Bipolar Disorder, but who knows? I hate the fact that I'm an emotional time bomb waiting to go off. The solution is simple. Just don't get pissed. Easier said than done. I'm not always this way. When things are going well and life is stable, the thoughts of death and irritability aren't all consuming. It's when things tend to slide off the beaten path that worries me. I wonder if this is a progressive disorder? I hope not.

I've dreamt that I've killed a room full of people with my fingernails and I wonder what road kill used to be and if I dissected it what parts would be missing. Revealing such intimate details about yourself leaves you feeling raw and vulnerable. If it helps someone else feel more "normal," I believe it's worth it though. Of course most people are capable of holding a grudge, becoming annoyed, swearing, giving a dirty look, or otherwise showing that they're peeved. Most folks don't feel the need to immediately prove a point, throw a tantrum, point out a difference in opinion, hold resentment, or seek revenge upon becoming upset, however. It's like the need to be unkind as a defense mechanism. After a while you grow a thick skin to whatever the world throws your way. We'd all be in trouble if everything got to us. One thing I hope I never become is a hunter though, to be so calm as to take the life of something just innocently breathing in front of me.

What's also scary is that I'm a step away from being schizophrenic. I don't hear voices telling me to do awful things or making me paranoid, but the thoughts of causing harm are there. It's terrifying enough when you think of hurting yourself. It's completely disconcerting when you think of anything homicidal. To have a disorder with which you are fixated with death is not fun.

I recall an instance where I became so irate at a telemarketer that I went off on him because he'd been the seventh person to call me for a particular promotion. I cussed and name-called and demanded that my name be taken off their call list "…especially since I told you people to stop calling me so many damn times before." If I could've reached through the phone to slap and strangle him I would've. I'm pretty sure this person had no way of knowing this and didn't deserve to be spoken to in that way (there was probably a whole call center of telemarketers being used and he was just the one who got my name that unfortunate day). It didn't matter to me. He simply got in my way.

I also recall trying to find a stylist to trim my hair one Sunday morning. It was past 11am so I figured everyone would be done with worship service if they attended. Little did I realize that stylists deserve a day off too! I called shop after shop leaving selfish messages like, "How do you expect to make money when you're not open!" and "It figures that you're not working today." I didn't know any of these folks personally and had no right to assume anything about them. Again, I didn't care. When

I did speak with one stylist who had a shop in her home, she said that she didn't have office hours on Sunday. What audacity! I promptly called her a bitch and hung up on her. Looking back, it's obvious that I was wrong.

I could go on to explain how controversy followed (or moreover was created) wherever I went. I thought life was just particularly hard for me. It may be hereditary? My maternal grandmother was conceived during an affair. This contributed to the belief that both she and I should've never been born. She was known for her resentment and how she mistreated people. She could be kind, although, it was far too seldom shown. I also have maternal aunts who threaten each other with bodily harm (they've slapped each other in front of their children and threatened different methods of killing one another) when tempers flair. Having been shown such examples of disregard for anyone else and using sarcasm along with having a lifeless affect is awful. It's not always been easy for people to approach me. For those who've tried and failed, I appreciate your efforts. For those who didn't try, I don't blame you. It's only too bad that you've had to suffer my attitude to begin with. Now you know why.

More Than One Treatment

My first suicide attempt was at twelve years old. My parents had just divorced and I had not yet come to terms with the fact that they were never going to be together again. The twenty years since then have been tumultuous. I didn't realize that it might be years between manic episodes. But they are definite and very telling.

Once, after being out-of-work for four months due to a bad decision on my part (I had given notice that I was quitting because a lack of grant funding meant I'd need to work part-time versus full — and often over-time with a great non-profit organization), I was hired to direct a consortium to prevent fetal alcohol syndrome. Before I had begun my first day of work, there was a holiday party that I attended. I was so exuberant over receiving the news about the job that I acted like a complete idiot in front of my peers and future supervisors. I laughed and cajoled so loud that people commented on hearing me across the ballroom! I was the life of my table, cracking inappropriate jokes with board members and making a mockery of the event (a skit was being performed to the audience). The program presenters must have been horrified! The next morning I thought they were going to call and rescind the job offer! Luckily my supervisors didn't give much weight to my behavior the evening before. It went on to be one of my favorite jobs ever. Unfortunately, it also ended due to a lack of grant funding.

Between the ages of twelve (the first time I was hospitalized for depression) and thirty-two (diagnosis) my primal development seemed to occur. What I mean, is, that what should have been developed much earlier in life was either underdeveloped or undeveloped. I can blame my folks for a lack of guidance all I want to. The truth is stranger than fiction though:

November 5, 2005

It's like pulling teeth to get Dad to open up about anything. There is seldom a straight answer given when he's asked even a direct question. He's mastered ambivalence, giving roundabout answers, and often-complete stoicism. For many reasons, his leisure time is spent drinking and driving. Not fast. But slowly and purposefully alone down many a country road.—Although, nobody drinks alone when they've got memories to keep them company.

I can't remember a weekend (or rarely a weekday) that Dad doesn't use alcohol, usually 3.2 beers. When things do seem to bother him, the hard stuff (whiskey, schnapps, or blackberry brandy) is in-hand.

Being the oldest of 8 children (all born within 10 years of one another) couldn't have been easy. He probably didn't get much one-on-one time with either parent. Growing up, not much was expected of Dad surprisingly. Responsibility wasn't discussed. According to him, you just did what you were told to do when you were told to do it. Love was assumed. It wasn't a word often used and it was sparingly shown besides Grandma giving the occasional hug and being kind with her voice. Grandpa kidded about taking the children "over one knee" but discipline was nil. Emotion of any sort seemed contained. Sure there was laughter, sadness, excited ness over a football game, etc. But true emotion was evaded. Only later in life has Dad learned how to show concern, interest, desire, or express gratitude. Manners were also non-existent. Grandma would chime in "bless your little heart" when someone burped or farted. Otherwise, please, thank-you, and excuse me just didn't exist. There is also uneasiness about meeting new people or an unsettling effect regarding change. It's probably because Dad moved so much during his childhood. Grandpa would get tired of a job and announce to Grandma, "Pack up, we're moving." And so she would. Mom, on the other hand, embraces meeting new people as a chance to impress/bedazzle them.

It's not surprising, then, that my brothers and I were assumed to be loved too. I'm certain Grandpa [Dad's Dad] didn't learn how to express love from his parents either. Who knows if the cycle was ever any different? Besides anger, resentment, competition, belittling and otherwise backstabbing, little positive expression was ever shown with my Mother and her immediate family either.

November 6, 2005
I'd mentioned before that Dad drinks and drives for many reasons. I believe it has to do with self-medication, lack of knowing how to express emotion, low self-esteem, stress, and being passive or too scared to try anything new. I could be off; hell, I know I'm off, but I could be all wet regarding what I think? Self-doubt is common these days. There are so many other ways to express how you feel, like music, dance, writing, painting, etc. Of course, there's also illicit drug use, violence, gambling, crime. Who's to say why we choose the vices we do? Sometimes it's easier to just be scatter-brained and have no outlet at all.

Highlights in my disorder include (but are not limited to): making grossly inappropriate comments, laughter at funerals (yes, plural), extreme condescension towards people I am no better than, sexual acts without conscious, unintentional cursing/outbursts of anger, multiple assumed expectations (it was shocking when I discovered that the world didn't revolve around me), feeling uncomfortable in my own skin, not listening to others because any instruction or direction being given was too slow for my racing mind, the need to dawdle on minor tasks regardless of who or what was waiting, very weird dreams on a nightly basis (before and after the mood stabilizers), bizarre compulsions/obsessions (like having people walk only on my right side or needing everything to be symmetrical), absent mindedness (as if it didn't matter whether I was paying attention or not), agreeing to whatever people were saying even though I had no clue what they were talking about, wanting to buy permanent items (furniture, pets, carpeting) for people without consulting with them first, proving my intelligence to strangers by repeating quotes (which were often misquotes) to make me seem more interesting, reading the first fifty-or-so pages of a book and never finishing it (hopefully that won't happen here!) even though I loved the book (there was no time to complete a task because I was already on to the next one), and the need to "set people straight." These are quirks that anyone could have with or without a mood disorder. Again, there's a pattern here that isn't pretty.—Defeatist and extremist attitudes can also be your downfall. Hope is powerful if you have it and essential if you don't. I'd blame myself for contributing to the many unfair and unkind acts in the world (female genital mutilation, world hunger, poverty, illiteracy, even infertility) because I'm doing nothing about it. *I could've been a surrogate mother. As a privileged person I have the power to do something about these awful things, but I don't…*The guilt and shame from indifference can eat you alive if you haven't got the will to survive it.

    I remember praying to God sometimes that I would lose my mind.

November 27, 2005

There are so many ways to commit suicide. The thoughts consume me. There is the obvious overdose, ingestion of something toxic, or strangulation. I could drive my car into something or off something, or just leave it parked in the garage running. I could take the more lethal routes of using a gun or knife through the vital organs (brain/heart) or slit my wrists. Or I could be creative, find an exposed electrical outlet, fall down a flight of stairs, starve myself, hit my head and drown in the bathtub...but then, if I really wanted to die, I'd already be dead.

December 10, 2005

The thoughts are still there. Maybe if I strangled the cat? She's really become a pest lately. We don't pay any attention to her and can't afford her so it'd be like saving her from loneliness and starvation. I drive by cemeteries and wonder how everybody died? Lucky bastards. If I was murdered and it was made to look like a suicide, would anyone investigate?

Did I mention I love cats? I can see the scattered thought process and how Bipolar Disorder makes me think things that I never would otherwise. Before treatment as an adult (diagnosis, therapy, medication, and recommendations), I truly didn't know how to feel. I was either giddy and would laugh nervously or hysterically after everything (even if it was a serious matter) or be a-symptomatic.

On the other hand, if you don't get your way, a suicidal threat can become a trump card versus an actual notice of intentional harm. Like a spoiled child though, it is so very important that I get my way. Thoughts of hopelessness/helplessness come on too easily otherwise.

Why Do You Need It?

There is very little "constructive" criticism when you're bipolar. You're either excellent or you suck. The truth is hard to hear sometimes. I married a man similar to my father, very frugal. My Dad teases newborns by looking at them and saying, "Can you say shit yet?" My husband, on the other hand, probably thinks about the cost of diapers every time the baby takes a shit. In any case, I used to enjoy shopping until I got to the point that I dreaded coming home from it. The questions would begin: "How much did you spend?" "How much was this?" "How much was that?" Then it would be: "You should've waited until it was on sale," "How can you justify spending that?" or "Why do you need it?" There was a point in time that we'd argue over why certain arbitrary items were bought (a particular brand of graham cracker for example). Shopping for pleasure soon gave way to shopping only for necessity.

Of course my husband had every right to worry about how the bills would be paid if I kept spending any money that was made. However, these questions weren't helping. My loving spouse wasn't familiar with how to communicate without shaming or blaming. It compounded feelings of guilt, hurt, and anger. Although I was just as much to "blame" as he was, it was awful for both of us to go through.

Compulsive shopping can give you such an emotional high though. Men often wonder why women have several pairs of shoes that look exactly alike except for their color. That's why! It can be exciting to have a collection of items few others will ever ascertain. Whether it is shoes, clothing, jewelry, dolls, knick-knacks, whatever, you get attention when you have something unique. Although, the trouble with BD is that it's an empty emotional high. You think you'll feel better having spent an exorbitant amount of money, but it only makes you feel worse.

Not only have you jeopardized your relationship with your partner, you're in debt, you've put your credit in peril, and it doesn't help you unless you can resell the items (and that's if you purchased items that could be resold)! – For instance, between unnecessary bleaching, veneers, crowns, and orthodontics, thousands of dollars were spent on my teeth when they were fine to begin with. Perfectionism has a price. What seemed so vital at the time of purchase is now a constant reminder of how much money I could've had. It's like people who become addicted to cosmetic surgery. Who *needs* it?

Hindsight is always 20/20. It's easy to pick on yourself and wonder why you did half the things you did after the fact. Everyone with a conscious has regret. It's a shame, though, that untreated people with BD don't realize it often until it's too late.

I remember being elated when there was over $100 in my checking account again. I'm quite susceptible to get-rich-quick schemes, infomercials, or work-from-home ventures. They sound so good! Reasonable expectations prevent most people from buying into such scams or "opportunities." I've peddled candy machines, baseball cards, baskets, encouraged website affiliation (where you profit from other people purchasing items from your website), and selling bargains by fax as well as submitted ideas for invention. All seem very promising until life happens. You need time, money, and commitment to run a successful business, regardless of whether or not it has a storefront. It's also easy to lose track of what you were doing because of racing thoughts (obviously not good for business). But then again, sensationalizing is common during mania.

You'd think I would've learned through the first or second failure. It's nice to be optimistic, but you'll go broke and become seriously depressed if you're not careful. If you really have a sense of responsibility, it can be crushing:

November 20, 2005

What is truly depressing is the fact that you can't afford a suicide attempt these days. Even though insurance pays 80%, that doesn't mean there aren't substantial costs involved between the ambulance ride, hospital stay, doctor's bill, treatment, and medication. Since I lived through it, I'm screwed. It seems so unfair that even after working 50-60 hours per week that we still need to decide which bills to pay. But it does no good to host a pity party. There's always some poor bastard who's worse off than you. Is this saying actually supposed to make you feel thankful or less selfish?

Talking yourself out of committing suicide again actually gets easier as the bills arrive (ironically).

The holidays also tend to bring out depression as well as generosity in many people. I'm no exception. I want to be helpful and feel useful. Like trying to donate to as many charities as possible. However, after being asked for support from the local law enforcement/fire fighters, neighborhood children (school and activity fund raisers), church, public television, various disease prevention organizations, food and clothing drives, and national as well as international disaster relief efforts, I feel a bit overwhelmed. I also seem to need to "help" by jumping into a conversation unwelcome (giving continuous suggestions), answering unsolicited e-mail and snail mail, or stopping on the freeway to assist a motorist even though the state trooper has arrived. *Is my need for redemption that great?* After a while, I began to question my own credibility towards doing good. With the increasing call to help the less fortunate I didn't realize that I was quickly becoming the less fortunate! The holiday season does funny things to people. Maybe one day I'll reminisce at the fact that we have to buy things only when they're on sale and rotate when we buy basic necessities? Until then, credit cards aren't essential and toothpaste is always on sale somewhere.

Really, Woman Isn't a Dirty Word?

Besides overspending money I don't have, I've done many things in my life that need atonement. On one end of the spectrum you have loss of interest in sex. On the other end you have the term hypersexual. Being hypersexual is a symptom of manic depression, or so I'm told. I just thought I was especially horny. Although it can be a lot of fun if you're in a committed relationship, it can get you into trouble if you're not. I remember having sex with guy's years ago just because they were there. After all, why does a bear shit in the woods? It didn't matter if a guy was attractive, clean, available, or even if he necessarily liked me. I'd flirt with someone who looked like an easy target. I'd use men who didn't seem to mind being used. Some did, however, and for them I apologize. I can honestly say I've never cheated on my husband and never will. It's scary to hear about those with BD who've gone astray from their spouse though.

It's unheard of for women to talk about their sex life openly, especially pre-marital. It's like picking your nose or masturbation. Everybody does it but nobody wants to talk about it. I don't mean any disrespect towards anyone. Maybe that's the difference between men and women? I feel the need to apologize. In any case, I have to consciously try not to put myself down for having fortuitous adventures. I'm envious of people who have the courage and conviction to remain virgins until either their wedding night or they become engaged/otherwise committed. The pressure is immense. Although it seems unrealistic for people to remain virgins too much longer after age 18, I imagine it is possible.

Because the word woman is treated like it's dirty and unusable in everyday conversation, it's also taboo to discuss a woman's libido. It's like a big secret no one wants to hear unless she's single and loose. If we don't talk about it, though, it sounds like men only have sex with each other or by themselves. And we know that's not entirely true…

Lie to Me

I'd never thought about the word relationship before treatment. Relationships, platonic or otherwise, were simply encounters with other people. Even though I have parents, siblings, a spouse, close friends, and associates to talk to it's hard to readily express myself...

Sunday, October 23, 2005

Chad and I don't know how to communicate. I "shoot from the hip" if I hear something I don't like and he has a tendency to interrupt and express his opinion, even if I don't ask for it. We don't even try to understand one another's point of view. I feel incredibly lonely and am feeling sorry for myself. Lately it's taken all I have not to leave [commit suicide]. I love our children more than life itself though. Without Chad, I don't feel like I have anyone I can rely on. I have friends I talk to but no one I trust. Chad's gone so much recently, working two jobs, because of my debt. I keep bringing the family further down. I've been too depressed to work with other kids or outside the home. It's actually worked out that way with the daycare children. I was supposed to have a neighbor girl begin once per week but her parents hired a nanny. My other daycare kids went elsewhere because of the extended maternity leave. Chad suggested I take a part-time job in the evenings, which sounds like a good idea...until it materializes. It'll be cold out soon, we'll be playing with the kids, and I'll have to go. Spencer still wakes up during the night and when the other three new kids come I'm going to be so tired. My friend is getting twin foster daughters and I'll be watching them twice a week as well as another 3 month old and the boys. There never seems to be enough money. I went to college so I wouldn't feel trapped. I don't exactly feel trapped now, however, I feel limited due to my low energy level and poor choices.

I know I should be more certain of myself. I have plenty to live for. On the other hand, I hate feeling this way. I truly wouldn't wish it upon my worst enemy. I pray the kids don't get this feeling from me! Depression is like having a constant weight on your shoulders and chest holding you down/back. Lately I've just failed to see how good I have it. Chad was upset this morning because he felt like he has to do everything around the house. He took care of the kids a few hours, started laundry, and vacuumed. I know he works long hours outside the home but I contribute too. Between the diaper changes, feedings, picking up toys, chasing around, dressing, reading, educating and otherwise entertaining the kids, I manage to fold laundry, unload/reload the dishwasher, clean the carpets, occasionally clean the bathrooms, make the beds, and restock supplies among other duties. Maybe I should offer to change the oil in the vehicles too?

I returned home [Faribault County] yesterday to look at an old farm site. I didn't tell Chad I was going because I didn't want to hear what he had to say about it. The house was built in 1910 and has been added onto. It needs major updating! I loved it. It sits on over 2.5 acres and is atop a hill. It has a three-stall garage attached to the house as well as a separate unattached one with a workshop. The property is less than half of what we currently owe on our home. It makes a huge difference what county you reside in! Anyways, I began to imagine how nice it would be to have the boys playing outside and to be by our parents again. The trouble is, by *the time you update the house (new shingles, carpeting, siding and windows, etc.), it brings you back up. The mortgage and taxes still wouldn't be what we're currently paying. ~ There are downsides too. We'd have to commute to wherever we needed to go (work, school, shopping, etc.) The kids would be in a consolidated school district. The elementary school may still be there for several more years? Who knows? For some reason I picture Chad driving truck and us being happy there. It's all-moot anyway. I can blame Chad all I want for diminishing my dreams or belittling how I feel, but the fact of the matter is I let him make me feel this way. He has just as much right to his way of thinking as I do mine. I just wish we were on the same page again.*

I have an appointment with Dr. Lombardo Tuesday. She's very kind. I imagine journaling has been just as therapeutic as seeing her. At least insurance pays the brunt of that bill. Lord knows I try to be good intentioned. But it usually backfires. It would be so nice if I were smarter.

The kids are finally sleeping. Spencer cried for an hour straight this evening. He had a big burp and then just wanted to be held. As long as he's being held he's fine. He rolled over for the first time this evening. Both he and Carter are growing up so fast!

Well, I suppose I should stop talking to myself and hit the hay. At least the Vikings won against Green Bay today as a consolation. I'm sure better days are yet to come.

Journaling can be very therapeutic if you let it. I'd often find me talking to myself in mirrors as well. I'd say, "At least today is better than yesterday," even if it wasn't. I needed that ego stroke and constant reassurance that everything is "normal" or would soon be "normal."

When I found myself particularly down, I'd say to Chad, "Lie to me, please." I just didn't want to feel like a failure and loser again that day. I was jealous of horses wearing blinders; At least they didn't see what was coming. Having such a sense of dread and doom can be weary. You become thankful for the symptoms of BD or your bipolar meds that you do have (loss of libido and weight gain) at that point. After our children were born I became even more self-conscious than usual about my appearance. I really needed Chad to lie to me then!

Finally, Diagnosis

I feel for those who either go undiagnosed or who are misdiagnosed. To question your own sanity is troubling, at best, horrible, at worst. I was diagnosed with manic-depression at an in-patient mental health unit of a local hospital the day after I'd attempted suicide. This time it was an overdose of acetaminophen. I'm not certain how often I've tried to commit suicide? I do know that I just wanted the pain to end.

It was less than six months after the birth of our second and youngest child (we decided a tubal ligation was appropriate at that point). We would have certainly gone on to have more children if not for my mental illness. I've met people who've decided not to have children at all due to the possibility of passing it on to any offspring. I digress...I was incredibly stressed with my job (home daycare) and was thoroughly sleep deprived. October 24, 2005 began like any other day, yet everything seemed wrong. I begrudgingly got the kids up, changed their diapers, fed and dressed them. The rest of the day I laid down and wanted to die. Three of my four immediate family members now lived out-of-state and I hadn't spoken to the one remaining in weeks (for no good reason). I was lonely and depressed. Not only did I not want to get back into daycare so quickly after having a baby, I wasn't certain I wanted to go back into it at all (there are certain professions that people with BD should stay away from, home daycare might be one of them.)

I kept going back and forth in my mind between the positives and negatives of staying at home "babysitting." The obvious reason for many providers is the fact that you get to be with your own children while earning an income. I was no exception. But there's so much more to it than that. No longer did I have to spend money on gas for commuting, I didn't have to wake the kids to go anywhere during inclimate weather, I could clean the house (or so I thought) when the kids were napping, and I could be my own boss. I enjoyed the laughter, group hugs, cooing, innocent confusion, and otherwise playfulness of kids too. After deciding to leave my job as the Director of Admissions and department head for a local nursing home, I went through the necessary training and completed the mountain of paperwork to begin doing licensed daycare. My former supervisor said, "You won't last six months!" He suspected my Type A personality would get the better of me. Although I managed to make it longer than six months, I was wishing at that point that I'd never started. I had been in the business about eighteen months when our youngest was born. Our niece, Katie, helped with the daycare children for the first seven weeks of maternity leave (thank God!) I thought I didn't need to take a break so I told my daycare parents to keep coming. After the initial two months, Katie went back to college from summer break and I was alone with four to six children (depending on the day) and my post-partum depression. Because I specialized in infant and toddler care, I wasn't able to go outside when I wanted to even if the weather was nice. I developed a serious case of cabin fever. There was also a lack of adult conversation. Unless a friend called me I didn't have the ambition to call anyone else. I was inundated with battery-operated toys, books, videos, and baby equipment. Along with sometimes filthy blankies and Nuks came the indecision of what to do with multiple crying children. The soiled clothing and messes on the carpet were an added treat. Between handing out fruit snacks, toilet training, finagling over a decent wage, and trying to relieve back, neck, and shoulder pain, there were always little fires to be put out. Someone was screaming because a toy had been taken away, someone else needing to be held or otherwise entertained, and someone else was fussing because they wanted a bottle. The incessant whining made me yearn for the day to end. I'd worry about any little sniffle from the kids because whatever they had would spread like wildfire throughout the daycare. Trying to keep track of one child's "binkie" was difficult enough. Searching for three or four was mind-boggling.

I'd tried so hard to turn my life around after having no conscious as a teenager that any infraction now came as a major setback. Not only were there food program forms piling up, it weighed on my mind that I was cited by the county for not having a tag on my fire extinguisher and for not having a bar of soap in my first aid kit. Ridiculous as it seems, these were great failures in my book. My dream of keeping an immaculate house went up in flames as well. There was little time for a bathroom break let alone cleaning the house! Being a self-proclaimed "neat freak," this didn't set well with me. There was also the obvious clean up of body fluids. Who knew that spit-up, puke, boogers, pee, and poop were so prevalent? Also, imagine having someone else's breast milk being thrown-up on you and having any remnants left to clean up in a runny diaper. This doesn't bother some providers at all (be sure to thank them if you have them!) I was tired of the piled up laundry and would repeatedly sing the theme songs to Sesame Street, Barney, Bob the Builder, Teletubbies, Boobah, Reading Rainbow, Between the Lions and Dragon Tales in my head to pass the time. Finally, the mere smell of baby food (amongst everything else) got to me. I thought, I have a graduate degree and made a decent living before daycare; now look at what my life has become. In retrospect, I'm grateful to have had the children as well as the parents I did to work with. It could have been so much worse! Daycare is one of the only legitimate work-at-home businesses out there. Even though I was highly recommended, I worked as a licensed daycare provider solely because I needed the money and wanted to stay home with my children. Because I was such a novice, taking care of my own kids would have been enough. I just wanted to feel like I was contributing to the household income more so than simply saving on having to pay for daycare if I worked outside the home. Although they were never neglected or in any danger, I believed that the kids in my care and their parents deserved better. After a nervous breakdown involving a child who'd smeared her feces inside the crib and all over herself, I decided to take a break from doing daycare. Within a few weeks, though, the feelings of guilt and shame from not earning money while being able-bodied contributed to my feelings of worthlessness. I thought, "Should I get a job outside the home? No, then the boys will have to be in daycare. They deserved so much better than me anyways. When I'm gone Chad will have enough insurance money to stay home with the kids or hire someone to take care of them." I looked in the closet where a bottle of bulk acetaminophen was kept and promptly downed a handful. I locked myself in the bedroom, crawled into bed and waited to die. Chad was home within a couple of hours. I was delirious at that point. The kids were crying and the house was a disaster. Chad tried to talk to me but I mumbled to him, "I don't care" and went and lay on the couch instead. He called his sister to come and get the kids and kept saying, "This isn't her."

After being rushed to the hospital, worrying my loved ones, ingesting muco-mist, and being transferred to a psych ward, one tends to have a different outlook on life. The thing about "cries for help" is that they give you opportunities like treatment. It's an opportunity to listen to others' stories and realize your own mistakes.

During my stay in treatment I was housed with other folks who'd tried to commit suicide, drug addicts, a very confused elderly woman, a derelict, and a schizophrenic. It's not that I thought that I shouldn't have been hospitalized, but with *these* people? I immediately began pointing out flaws. First with the building, then the staff, and then with any policies and practices that I didn't like. I remember being very angry that I survived. I was quite tired and had a flat affect. Otherwise, I began looking for ways to try and kill myself again. *I could try to starve myself, poke my temple with a pen, stick a wet finger into a light socket, strangle myself...* It was then that I realized I was truly a basket case.

My first evening there I was in a padded room with a bolted-down bed and a video camera staring at me. In the morning a friendly Dr. Wilson came to speak with me. I told him about my extremes in mood. First flighty and uncaring, then gravely depressed. I didn't know there were any other emotions besides anger. I smiled but didn't *feel* happy. Within five minutes of talking with me, Dr. Wilson suggested Bipolar Disorder. He recommended a video; *Dark Glasses and Kaleidoscopes* as well as one other I don't remember the title of and the book, *An Unquiet Mind: A Memoir of Moods and Madness*. After seeing the videos, reading the book, and attending daily group sessions, a light bulb seemed to go off in my head. It all became so clear. I was relieved to have finally gotten the answers to my questions: Why am I so moody? Why don't I seem to care about anything? Why do I behave so odd [manic]? — Then another flood of questions came: Did I inherit this? Will my children inherit this? Will my family (particularly my husband and children) forgive me for trying to commit suicide? Will I be committed to an institution? What now?

Surprisingly, Dr. Wilson said we'd shoot for Friday to have me back home. What?! I wanted to die on Monday and he's saying I'm "cured" by the end of the week? Little did I know that Dr. Wilson knew what he was talking about. I was far from cured, nor would I be any time soon. But with the outpatient plan they established for me, things would progress better if I was at home rather than in the hospital. In treatment I began taking a mood stabilizer as well as my already prescribed Prozac. I was encouraged to express how I feel (if I was able to), I met a great friend, and I was taught to set goals for myself. I was able to realize that I truly didn't want to die. I also wrote a list of things I needed to be worried about or was scared of. They included:

- Being overwhelmed with questions (where've you been?)
- Over-reacting to minor situations
- Becoming jittery/agitated with the kids (or anything for that matter)
- Money worries
- People treating me differently if they find out where I am and what I've done
- Fighting with Chad [spouse]
- Long-term physical effects of the suicide attempt [acetaminophen overdose]
- Lost time with family
- Imposing upon extended family to watch children during treatment
- Catching up on household duties
- Side effects of new drug (Risperdal)
- Being trusted/taken seriously

The odd thing is, other than a few family members; no one knew I was gone. I had friends who called during the week, but my husband evaded their questions beautifully and excused my absence. Upon my return home I explained away my "nonexistence" by telling people that I was at a conference or visiting a friend from out of town. Of course I was attending group conferences and I was the "friend" that was being visited. Although my list of concerns were legitimate, regret is only good if you learn from it. I received the benefit of people's trust whether I was worthy of it or not. It's a reciprocity. I believe I'd now learned from my regret.

It's All-Good

The days preceding my release from the hospital, promises were made to and from me. After treatment, it's all-good at first. The day after I came home from the psych ward was bliss:

October 29, 2005

...We made love and held one another tight. We made promises about how we would treat each other and repeatedly thanked each other for the other's existence...

Then the kids woke up. We began taking each other for granted almost immediately. We under-appreciated each other's efforts. I began to feel selfish for wanting to do anything non-child-related (sleep deprivation definitely gets the better of you). Everybody wants a piece of you when your title is Mom.

They say having children changes everything. Whoever "they" are, they're right! Unless you have a nanny, personal trainer, chef, housekeeper, and the time to train or otherwise utilize these staff, life changes with children. Stress (even positive stressors) on any level can alter anyone's mood. With a mood disorder, however, I believe you question your ability to parent more often than most. Not only are children financially draining, they can bring out emotions that you didn't realize you had. Pulling my hair out would've been less painful than watching my own children as well as the children in my daycare exhibit my response to frustration (pouting, screaming, brooding, throwing things, name calling, etc.)

Because the income was essential I took on two new part-time daycare children. I felt helpless due to self-consciousness and would scare myself with my reaction to minor incidents (the toddlers would pull the chairs out from the kitchen table and I'd follow them around pushing them back in until finally I'd holler at them to stop until they cried). I truly didn't know I had it in me. Unfortunately you don't realize the consequences of your response to anger until children demonstrate it for you.

After a while I became resentful of life in general. Along with stress and frustration, I projected mixed emotions from second-guessing myself so often. There were also daily "when are you coming home?" phone calls to my husband when things became unbearable or were getting to be too much. Suicidal thoughts lingered. This time, however, I kept hearing something a therapist who'd been assigned to me while I was in the hospital had said: "You no longer have the right to try to kill yourself. Your children will never recover from it. I've known people in there 50's who are still troubled by a parent's suicide." With that in mind, I began to think maybe I should take my children with me should I try again.

That was a definite wake-up call. Why was I trying to spite this oblivious therapist? [If I had a choice in the matter, I certainly wouldn't choose to think these thoughts!]. I can see now that she had a point, however, you have to be truly ill to think the way I was at that point in time. My children are so precious to me. I want for them everything I wasn't able to have and I want them to accomplish everything that I never will. It's scary to think what mania and depression have in store for me. This therapist assumed I have control over these terrible thoughts popping into my head (she did not specialize in Bipolar Disorder). After finding a different therapist, I now look forward to attending regular sessions. At least with medication and proper treatment I'm better able to control the outcome.

What Have I Done?

Honesty is always the best policy, right? That doesn't mean I wasn't petrified to tell my husband about my thoughts of both grandeur and of suicidal/homicidal contemplations. Especially since I'd just gotten out of treatment a few weeks prior.

December 1, 2005

I went to see Dr. Lombardo today. What a weight off my shoulders that was! I mentioned I didn't want to return to the therapist I'd been assigned to while I was in the hospital. Dr. Lombardo is the most professional doctor I've ever met. She didn't try to excuse or defend the previous therapist or her comments. Instead, she listened thoughtfully to why I didn't want to return. She also said something that seems obvious; though, I hadn't thought about it before. She said that therapy shouldn't make you feel worse. I knew I wanted to feel better but that hit home. She also mentioned that goals should be established. This made sense. Otherwise, there'll be no end in sight.

I told Chad this evening about my thoughts from last weekend of taking the kids with me should I ever try suicide again. Of course he was shocked. So was I! I'd never want to intentionally hurt my children. It's then that I realized how serious a condition BD is. It's one thing to want to harm myself. But when anyone else is involved, especially my children, that's huge.

I'd mentioned before that regret is a powerful emotion. Along with consistent non-intentional thoughts of suicide, I find myself scratching my head at things I've done in the past…

I remember talking with a man who chaired a support group for people who'd lost their children through death. He said that this wasn't a group anyone should have to be a part of. My response was, "That's for sure!" It wasn't said in a positive light, rather in a contrite, you big loser, type of way. It was during a manic phase in which I was high on attention simply from being the facilitator of a meeting that was about to take place.

I also recall the first time my mother met my then boyfriend, now husband, Chad. At some point in time everybody is embarrassed by something his/her parent has done. Sometimes I try to imagine a time when I haven't been embarrassed. In any case, Chad and I've been dating since I was sixteen years old. We'd just started seeing each other at the time. I lived with my father. Mom had a habit of showing up unannounced. We went outside and spoke with her as she sat in her car. I introduced them and she pretended to have known him since he was "this high" (holding her arm out for measurement). She went on to talk about how she knew his parents when he was born. I wanted to crawl in a hole and die. The trouble is, she knew she'd never met him or his parents before but kept on about how she had spent time with them. Instead of confronting her, I simply brushed it off and quickly changed the subject. Chad was too nice to say anything otherwise. There are reasons Mom didn't meet Chad's parents until we were three and a half years into our relationship. Bless her heart. Now I understand why she just wanted to be liked.

I don't know if I'll ever understand why I have the tendency to brush off certain things while other times I have to be right, regardless of who or what is to blame? I do know that I've done many an absent-minded thing in the past and will have to look forward to wondering about myself many times in the future.

Life After Treatment

I tended to question my own purpose for existence quite often. It meant nothing that I was a sister, wife, mother, etc. I remember thinking, "Maybe I'm just convincing myself that I have something that I don't?" Yet, the more I read about BD and the more I began to know myself, there is no question.

Once I returned home I did a little investigating. If you're insecure with knowing you have Bipolar Disorder or are in denial in any way, it's not easy to do research in your local library. Not only is mental health taboo to talk about, if you live in a smaller community, the librarian is probably your neighbor. Also, if the library does have books on manic depression, they're usually amongst those on schizophrenia and non-fiction work from psychotherapists. What I found in our library is rather new. The oldest book was written less than fifteen years ago (although there is previous work.) Other than "Electroboy" from Andy Behrman and "A Brilliant Madness: Living with Manic-Depressive Illness" by Patty Duke and Gloria Hochman, most of the books were written from a professional's perspective. Of course Redfield Jamison's "An Unquiet Mind," has both aspects. There were books that specialize further towards Bipolar Disorder and children – which is wonderful for those of us who suspect heredity will rear its ugly head. Still others were written for those who have to deal with those of us with manic depression. What I didn't see were many books with real perspective from regular people (non-celebrities, non-professionals).

I do like the advice from Miklowitz's "The Bipolar Disorder Survival Guide: What You and Your Family Need to Know" [Guilford Press, 2002, p. 64] of a self-administered checklist of both your personality traits and manic/depressive symptoms though:

WHAT'S ME AND WHAT'S MY ILLNESS?
Check as many of the following as apply.

Your personality traits   **Your manic depressive symptoms**

Your personality traits	Your manic depressive symptoms
_____ Reliable	_____ Euphoric
_____ Conscientious	_____ Grandiose
_____ Dependable	_____ Depressed
_____ Indecisive	_____ Loss of Interest
_____ Assertive	_____ Sleeping too much
_____ Open	_____ Sleeping too little
_____ Optimistic	_____ Racing thoughts
_____ Sociable	_____ Full of Energy
_____ Withdrawn	_____ Doing too many things
_____ Ambitious	_____ Highly distractible
_____ Aloof	_____ Feeling suicidal
_____ Critical	_____ More easily fatigued
_____ Intellectual	_____ Unable to concentrate
_____ Affectionate	_____ Irritable
_____ Spirited	_____ Feeling worthless
_____ Passive	_____ Taking big or unusual risks
_____ Talkative	_____ Wired
_____ Seeking novelty	_____ Highly anxious
_____ Spontaneous	_____ Slowed down
_____ Boisterous	_____ Sped up
_____ Fearful	_____ Overly goal-driven
_____ Pessimistic	_____ Aggressive impulses
_____ Erratic	_____ Hopeless
_____ Rebellious	_____ Unusually passive

Even with such tools, it can be difficult to determine the difference between what your personality holds as apposed to your disorder. You might have personality traits of being giddy, silly, and scatterbrained but you change when, during a manic phase, you have racing and grandiose thoughts. The waters can muddy in a hurry. I recommend reading as much as possible on the subject and taking into account that there is more than one type of manic depression.

In reading "New Hope for People with Bipolar Disorder" *[Jan Fawcett, et. al., Prima Publishing, 2000, p. 43]*, I see that there are several categories of BD as well as different subtypes. I most generally relate to Bipolar Disorder, Type II:

> *The diagnosis of bipolar II disorder is frequently missed due to its subtleties. It is characterized by episodes of hypomania alternating with even longer periods of major depression that can be very severe and threatening. Although these people exhibit symptoms that are commonly recognized as "abnormal" by either the patients or their families, their symptoms are generally not severe enough to mandate hospitalization, even though there may be some interference in their normal level of functioning. However, these patients do not manifest psychosis and may not even recognize, or report, their symptoms of hypomania, choosing only to remember their depressive episodes.*

It's interesting to note, though, that there are times when I have symptoms from other types; however, none are to the extreme suggested in other readings.

It's also helpful to be aware of the signs of depression and symptoms of suicidal ideation. Many professionals use the following signs as a gauge for depression *(Available: http://www.webmd.com/content/Article/87/99351.html)*:

- Emotions: Do you feel ineffably sad or cry a great deal?
- Appetite/weight: Have you gained or lost weight? Do you binge or overeat?
- Sleep: Do you have chronic insomnia or excessive sleepiness? Are you tired all the time, regardless of how much sleep you get?
- Anger: Do you experience outbursts of complaints or shouting? Have you been feeling resentful and angry?
- Outlook: Have you lost interest in hobbies or activities that you formerly enjoyed?
- Libido: Have you lost interest in sex?
- Self-esteem: Do you feel worthless, unattractive, and inappropriately guilty?
- Concentration: Do you have a hard time concentrating? Are your thoughts muddy or foggy?
- Anxiety: Do you brood; have phobias, delusions, or unfounded fears?
- Restlessness: Do you have trouble sitting still?
- Muted affect: Do you have slow body movements and speech?
- Suicide: Have you thought you'd be better off dead?

Fawcett, et al. *[2000, Prima Publishing, p. 137]* cite the following questions as helpful in determining suicidal risk:

- Do you feel hopeless about life, or sometimes feel like life is too painful to continue living?
- Are you suffering from constant worry, anxiety attacks, and/or the inability to sit still?
- Are you fearful of the future, and do you have episodes of pacing?
- What are your reasons for living at this point?
- Do you have any thoughts of dying or of ending your life?
- Have you attempted suicide in the past, or have you acted self-destructively on impulse?

- Do you have a suicidal plan?
- Do you have the means to carry it out (e.g. a gun, a high balcony)?

If you have two or more signs of depression for more than two weeks or have any suicidal notions, please seek professional help immediately. It can make a world of difference! I won't say that everything is better and there's nothing more to worry about, but talking to a trained professional has the potential to change your life.

Thankful

Now I'm not saying that Laura Ingalls Wilder was bipolar, but if she were I'd feel for her. See, back in her day she didn't have the availability of the medicines we do today or the right to refuse them if she so chose (not that this is a good idea). Even if the medicines were available, she might not have been able to afford them. My point is this; if you are diagnosed with Bipolar Disorder, count your blessings. We live in a time where people can be diagnosed with a disorder that is known and studied. We have the option and availability of taking medication to ease the symptoms, and we have mental health professionals to help us along the way. And, if you're unable to afford the medicines (as many people are), there are programs available to assist people in need. Being diagnosed with Bipolar Disorder doesn't have to be a death sentence. I can only imagine the frustration I'll encounter because of it. I can wonder all I want to why I have BD, but it won't help. The fact of the matter is that according to the National Institute of Mental Health, about 1 out of every five people has mental illness *(Available: http://www.webmd.com/content/Article/85/98464.html)* and I'm one of them. But I do know that with the right tools (meds, therapy, proper diet, familial/friend's support), I have a decent outlook and the chance to live a great life.

There are probably those who believe that folks with Bipolar Disorder are a group of weirdoes who've convinced themselves they have something that isn't real. Let me assure them, it's real! There are also some practitioners who believe that therapy alone should alleviate BD symptoms. I liken this to irresponsible treatment. If you have the means to provide appropriate care, then do it! Prescribing and providing medications aren't a luxury to patients with manic depression; they're a necessity. You can make the comparison to people who use any other medicine for a physical ailment. No one should have to suffer a bipolar person's attitude because of an innate chemical imbalance or an oblivious therapist.

In conclusion, repetition, schedules, and consistency are necessary for those of us who live with manic depression. Here's mine as an example:

Daily Schedule Monday-Friday
5:30am – Diaper change and bottle for baby when needed
6:30-7am – Wake (if not already), shower, dress, eat breakfast
7-7:45am – Feed & dress toddler, change diaper/encourage use of potty, brush teeth, clean-up kitchen
7:45-8am – Greet daycare children & parents
8-10am – Scheduled activity w/kids (games, movie, crafts, etc.)
10am – Snack, clean-up kitchen
10:30-11am – Free play for kids, phone calls/check e-mail
11am-Noon – Make & eat lunch, clean-up kitchen
Noon-1pm – Activities w/children, story-time
1pm – Clean-up toys, quiet-time
1:30-3:30pm – Exercise/household chores, relax (children nap)
3:30-4pm – Snack, clean-up kitchen
4-5:30pm – Free play w/kids
5:30-7pm – Make & eat supper, clean-up kitchen
7-8pm – Give baths when necessary, brush teeth, clean-up toys, read bedtime story
8-10pm – Bedtime for kids (8pm), watch tv/journal/read, visit w/ Chad, relax
10pm – Lights out

Activities & Meal Schedule

	Lunch	Supper
Monday – Movie/free play	Sandwich	Pork
Tuesday – Craft	Pasta	Chicken
Wednesday – Game	Hamburger	Pasta
Thursday – Educational	Eggs	Sandwich
Friday – Free play/movie	Pizza	Steak
Saturday – Pre-scheduled	Open	Eat-out
Sunday – Church/family-time	Brunch/eggs	Hotdish/left-overs

Like an addict, it's a struggle everyday to be free from impulses that would adversely affect me as well as so many others. You may think you're good at hiding items you've purchased and sometimes emotions (if you're able to have them), but people aren't fooled. I don't know if the (what I call minor) suicidal tendencies will ever go away? But I do know that taking Fluoxetine (Prozac) and Risperidone (Risperdal) has changed my life for the better. I was upset initially because I thought I might have to be on these medicines forever. After living through the extremes of Bipolar Disorder however, I now say, "So what!" Taking a pill or two a day and dealing with the potential side effects are much easier than battling the constant thoughts and feelings of manic depression. Seeing a therapist regularly and taking medication contributes to my mental health and I shouldn't be ashamed or be made to feel ashamed because of that.

I've finally gained purpose. It's one thing to have roles you play in life (wife, mother, daughter, sister, aunt, friend, etc.). It's entirely different to find out what it would be like not having you in your loved ones lives. I'm grateful the Lord channels His energies through humans. Maybe it's my grandeur thinking again? —*I wonder if there is an assembly of higher powers who consult with God or if we all worship one God and He's called different things (Allah, Buddha, etc.)? No matter.*

I'm also thankful I can show emotion and express love. You take for granted the simple things in life (laughter, choices, basic necessities) when you don't know how to feel. Maslow definitely knew what he was talking about when he created his *Hierarchy of Needs*! It seems cliché' that you don't realize pleasure without pain, but it's true. It's obvious to those without BD that your attitude can change from more than just immense pleasure to debilitating pain. You're able to give compliments without seeming contrite and the world is just plain different.

What I have learned from being hospitalized for manic depression is to take not just one day at a time, but one instance/activity/moment at a time. It's so easy to clutter things together and try to do everything at once in the interest of time. I might be slower than a turtle now (not that I was all that fast to begin with), but I tend to get things done. I'm also thankful for people who know about my Bipolar Disorder and don't treat me differently as a result. I loved hearing, "You're still cute; you just have shorter hair" from my husband after lopping off almost a foot of it. I'm just trying to like myself. Luckily, people with BD give others who are trying to help them a greater sense of purpose too. I can see now why God creates people with special needs. It isn't necessarily to benefit the people who have them, but to teach others around them just how good they have it.

Post Script

Throughout each chapter there is an aspect of agony that has since been replaced with hope, healing, and happiness. I was hesitant to tell my parents that I was writing this book because I was scared of how they might react. The relationships you don't want to jeopardize most besides your spouse or children is your parents. I was pleasantly surprised to hear, "make yourself happy" from my father and "you shouldn't care so much what we think" from my mother after showing them each specific chapters. Sometimes the anticipation is worse than the actual event. What I do want my parents to know is that they definitely have not done everything wrong, despite how it may sound. I remember great birthday parties thrown by Mom and learning how to ride my bike with Dad. There were also countless nights of worry, staying up with me while I was sick, making meals to comfort me, helping with homework, and encouraging a post-secondary education, amongst the many other things done right. This process has helped me to see that nobody's perfect and that my parents are human. Thank you Mom and Dad for understanding.

References

Behrman, A. (2003). *Electroboy: A memoir of mania.* New York: Random House.

Dark glasses and Kaleidoscopes: Living with manic depression. [videotape]. Narrated by Tony Dow. 1997. DBSA. 33 minutes.

Duke, P., & Hochman, G. (1992). *A brilliant madness: Living with manic-depressive illness.* New York: Bantam.

Fawcett, J., Golden, B., & Rosenfeld, N. (2000). *New hope for people with bipolar disorder.* New York: Prima Publishing, Pp. 43 & 137.

Kaplan, E.F., MD, & Turkington, C. (2001). *What is depression?,* reference from Making the antidepressant decision. WebMD [on-line].
Available: http://www.webmd.com/content/Article/87/99351.html.

Miklowitz, D.J., (2002). *The bipolar disorder survival guide: What you and your family need to know.* New York: The Guilford Press, p. 64.

Redfield Jamison, K. (1996). An unquiet mind: A memoir of moods and madness. New York: Vintage.

Zamora, D. (2004, April). Are mental illnesses becoming more prevalent, or is psychiatry overdiagnosing? WebMD [on-line].
Available: http://www.webmd.com/content/Article/85/98464.html.

Notes

Printed in the United States
51223LVS00006B/632